M3 Mathematics
MAPPING MATHEMATICAL MEANING

Fractions

Helen Pengelly

GW00602776

ASHTON SCHOLASTIC
SYDNEY AUCKLAND NEW YORK TORONTO LONDON

The purchase of this book entitles the teacher to reproduce
the blackline masters for classroom use.

First published in 1991 by Ashton Scholastic Pty Limited A.C.N. 000 614 577,
PO Box 579, Gosford 2250. Also in Brisbane, Melbourne, Adelaide, Perth and
Auckland, NZ.

Typeset by David Lake Typesetting, Forresters Beach NSW.
Printed by Globalcom Pty Ltd, Singapore.
Typeset in Helvetica.

12 11 10 9 8 7 6 5 4 3 2 1   1 2 3 4 5 / 9

Setting the context

This book is one in a series of books addressing mathematics curricula in the primary school years. Collectively, the books outline an approach to the teaching and learning of mathematics. Their purpose is to inform, support and resource teachers when planning, implementing and reviewing their mathematics programs.

Giving information about the rationale, content and methodology in a conceptual rather than a procedural way enables teachers to build a curriculum which is responsive to the needs of individual children, the class, the school and the school community. The materials do not provide a program in the traditional sense of setting learning out in a linear and prescribed manner through student books and teacher guides. They do provide teachers with a framework to build a mathematics curriculum which reflects the rationale and methodology of the different education department policy guidelines. Learning mathematics becomes a personal, interactive process negotiated between the policy statements of the institution and the school, the interests, abilities and reactions of the children in a class, and the teacher's belief, knowledge and practices.

One book discusses the principles underlying this approach to mathematics teaching. Six topic books give an account of these theories in action. They describe the nature and type of activities which give children personal experiences with mathematics. The books outline an ongoing process of planning for and responding to children's mathematical learning.

In another collection of books in this series, a group of teachers write about how they implemented this approach. Their books on getting started, on planning and programming, on assessment, evaluation and reporting, and on the role of language and interaction in mathematics learning, are practical accounts of organisation and management strategies. Books in the fourth category are to be used to resource students' mathematical learning in an active way.

How to use
Fractions

Fractions have always been considered difficult to learn. Children have trouble comprehending the values the fraction numerals represent. Many of the procedures for computing fractions appear complex and are inconsistent with the rules used for operating on whole numbers. When you multiply a quantity by a proper fraction, for example, you end up with a number which is less than the original number. Conversely, dividing a number by a fraction generates a result which is more than the starting number. This does not fit with children's existing knowledge about multiplication and division. Rules for operating on fractions seem complicated.

When fractions are explored as a way of expressing the relationships between various objects the concept, rather than the language, is the focus of a child's experience. In an experiential context, the notion of part–whole relations is not difficult for even quite young children to grasp. On the other hand, couching fraction concepts in symbols causes a great deal of confusion. In order to learn about fractions, children need extensive experiences exploring them as relationships between objects. They must also develop their own ways of representing fractions before formal symbols and operations are introduced. Fractions are only difficult to understand when they are seen as symbols to be manipulated, rather than ideas to be conceptualised.

Children gain an understanding of fractions by using materials to explore part–whole relationships. Giving children access to their own sets of materials is important. It enables them to form and check ideas that are relevant to them. In the beginning it is advisable to use materials that are easy to manipulate, namely wooden blocks, foam shapes and other sets of commercially available materials. As the mathematical ideas become established, and as motor skills develop, children will be able to work with the more compact shapes this book provides. Activities with these materials model fractions and the arithmetic procedures for operating on them.

This book consists of a series of shapes to be photocopied and cut out to make fraction sets. There are five basic shapes—a circle, a square, a diamond, a hexagon and a ten centimetre square. Each one of these base shapes is duplicated several times and divided into different sized parts which relate to the parent shape. The first four basic shapes deal mainly with common fractions, halves, thirds, quarters and fifths. The last one, the ten by ten square, replicates Base Ten material and is for exploring decimal fractions—tenths, hundredths, thousandths and eventually decimals.

Selected pages can be photocopied to form fraction sets. All the pieces that relate to the circle, for example, form one set. These pieces have been drawn so that they can be cut out and used as models for children to manipulate. It may be best to photocopy them onto card, as the thickness of cardboard makes it easier for children to handle.

Each child should have their own set of materials to work with. The task to begin an investigation of fractions might be, 'Give the largest block in your set the value of one. Find the value of all the other pieces. Record.' This activity can be repeated with other sets. The label given to a block is not to be thought of as a static description of the block itself, but a statement about its relationship to other blocks in the set. To this end, children change the block which is given the value of one and compute the values of all the other blocks.

When children can determine the relative values of different blocks within sets with ease, have them find different ways to make one (or a half, or three-quarters, or two, or . . .). This is a forerunner for work with equivalent fractions and for finding a rule for adding fractions. How children develop these understandings is described in a book in this series called *Making sense of **Fractions***.

When children's recordings of fractions are conventional, they can be challenged to find a rule for adding the numerals. In the first instance, ask children to find a rule for adding fractions which are the same size. After reviewing their recordings they find that 'the bottom number stays the same and you add the top numbers together'. This rule only works when the denominators are the same.

Once children are competently generating fractions that are equivalent, they use this knowledge to find out how to add fractions of different denominators. They realise that they have to make the fractions relate to the same base before it is possible to add them. To do this they find a multiple which is common to all of the base sizes of the fractions to be added. Equivalent fractions, using this new number as the base, are found for the original fractions. These fractions can now be added. The sum of the numerators indicates the size of the total. While this may seem a complex procedure, it has meaning for children because it develops out of their understandings.

Children come to these conclusions from their own experiences of manipulating materials, collecting data, looking for patterns, forming conjectures and refining them until a satisfactory conclusion or definition is reached. Teachers can assist this process by using their knowledge of fractions to create the examples and counter examples for children to reflect on.

Knowledge of the rules for adding fractions makes expanded notation of decimals into the sum of decimal fractions possible to comprehend.

Decimal fractions

The ten by ten grid and the accompanying shapes give children experiences with tenths and hundredths. Before using these shapes, children may find it easier to manipulate blocks that also model these decimal relationships. Knowing fractions and, in particular, decimal fractions, helps children understand decimals. This is described more fully in the books *Making sense of* **Fractions** and **Base Ten**, *understanding the structure of the number system*.

With decimal currency and metric measures now standard, there is less need for children to develop the explicit procedures required for computing fractions and there is a reduced emphasis on fractions in current curriculum materials. Nevertheless, a basic understanding is still essential if children are to understand numbers less than one and the numeration system.

It also helps children when they learn algebra. The rules for operating on algebraic symbols that are expressed as a ratio of two unknowns use the same rules as those used for operations on fractions.

More advanced students enjoy the challenge of collecting data, looking for patterns and establishing the rules for multiplying and dividing fractions.

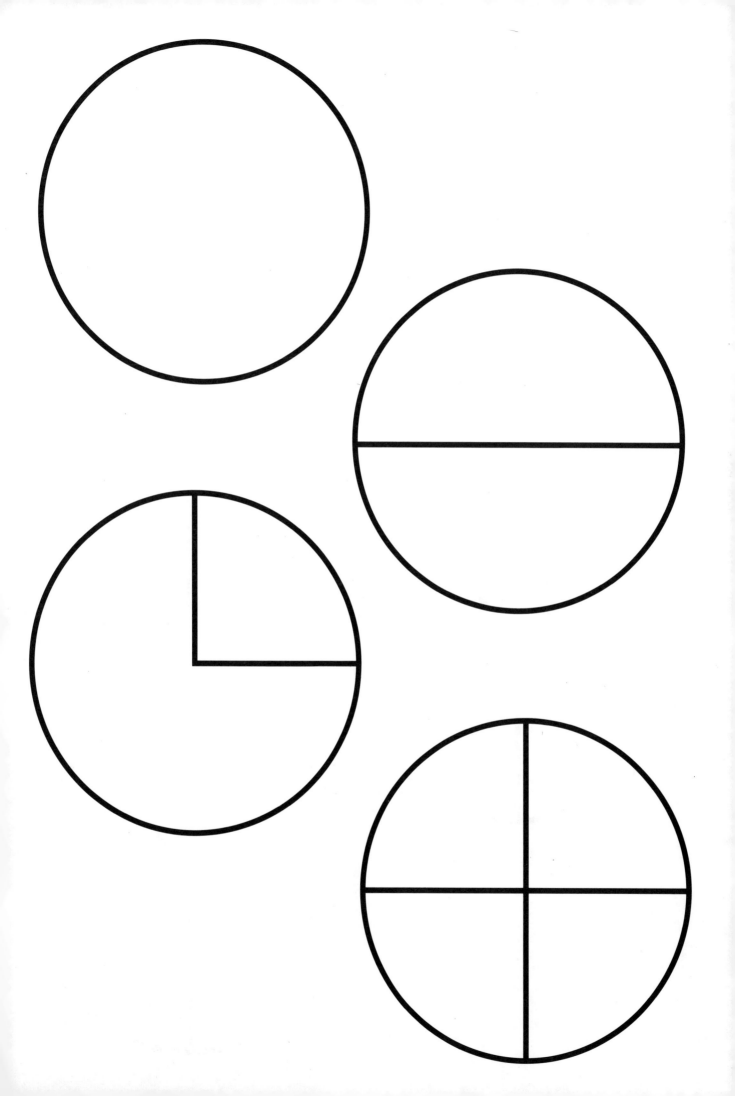

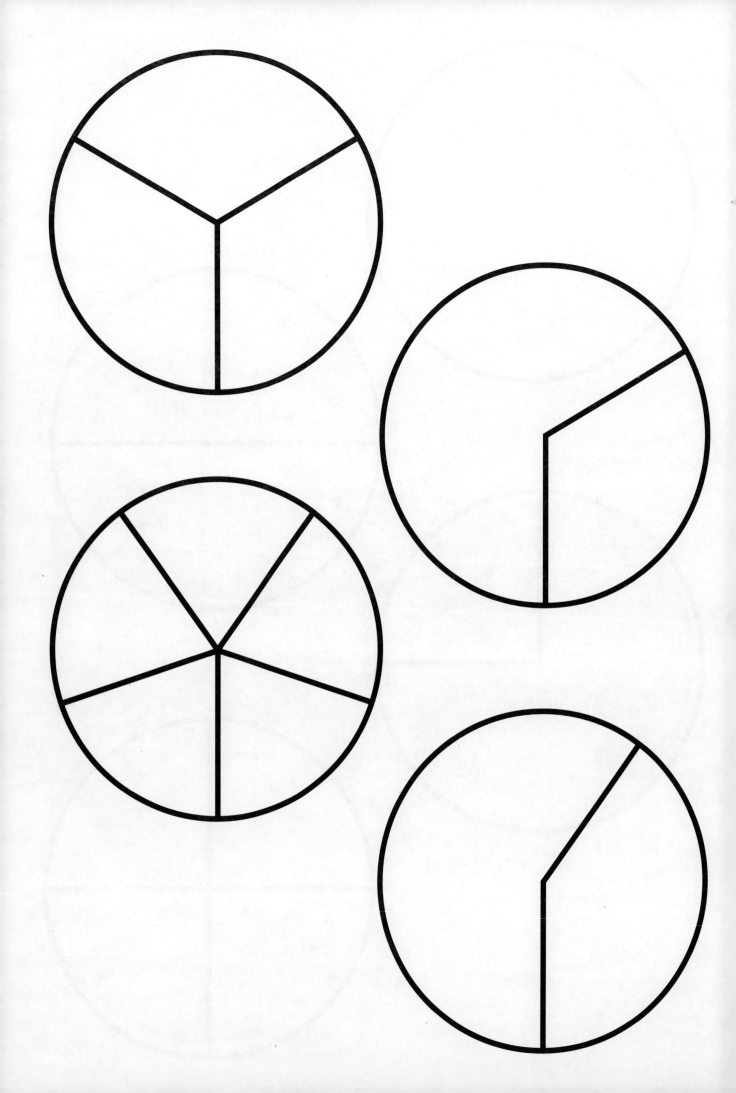

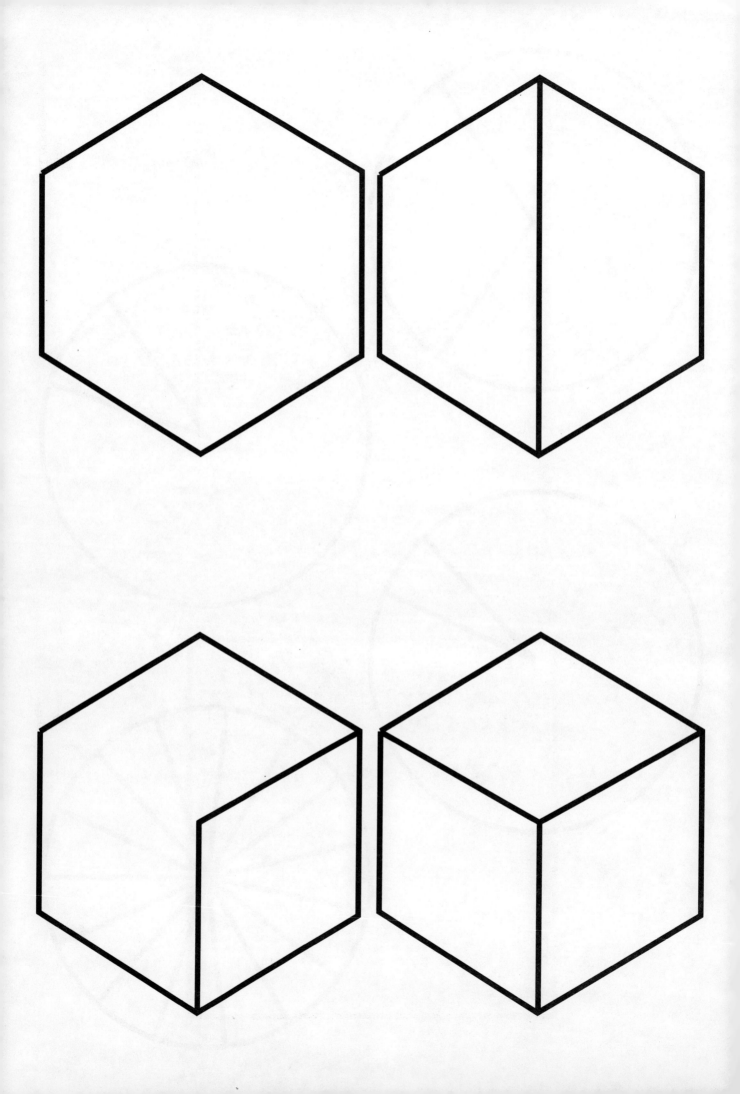

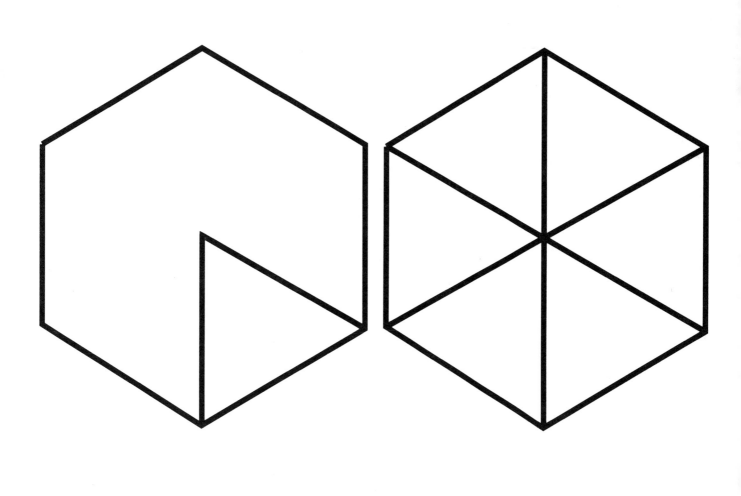
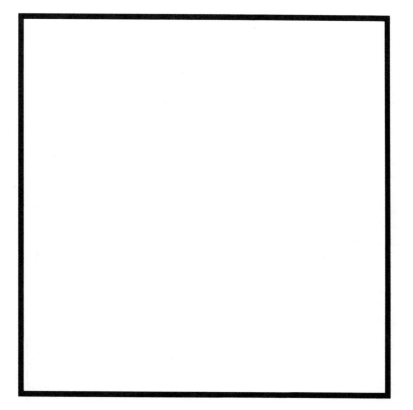

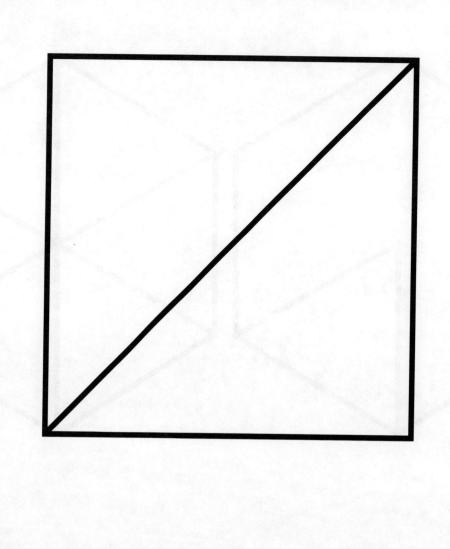

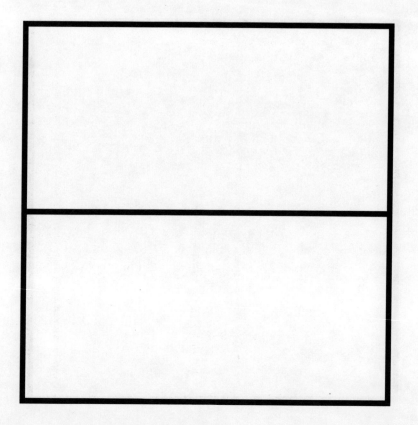

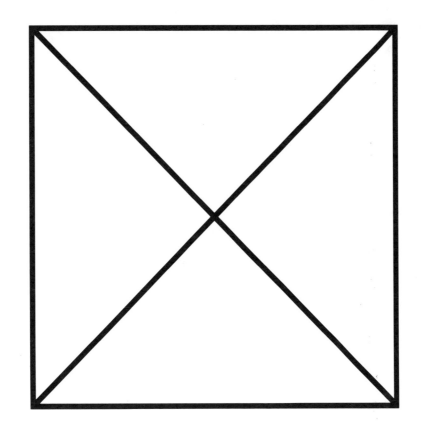

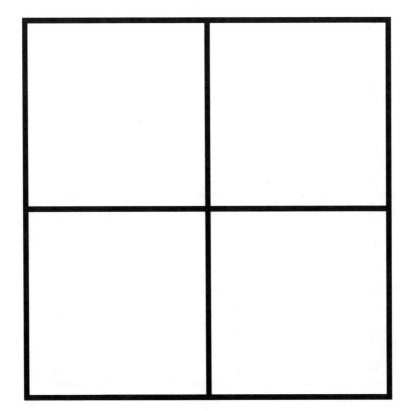

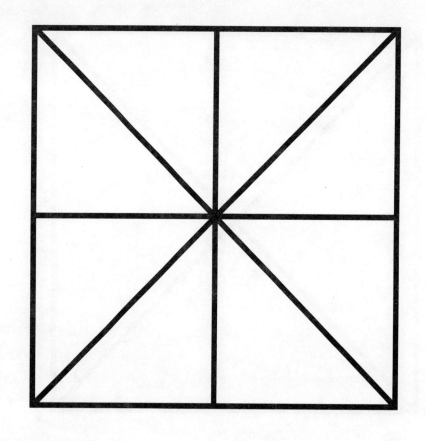

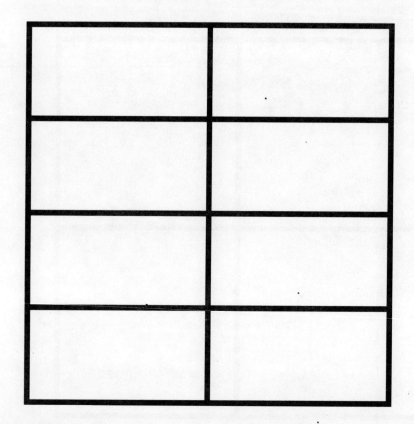

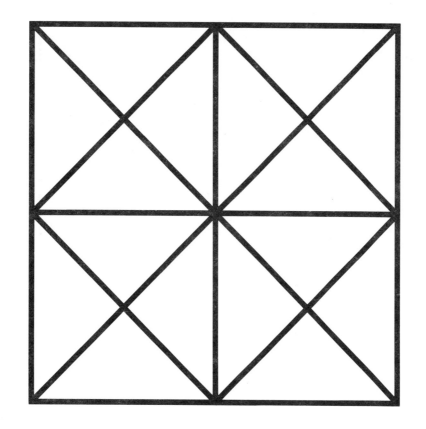

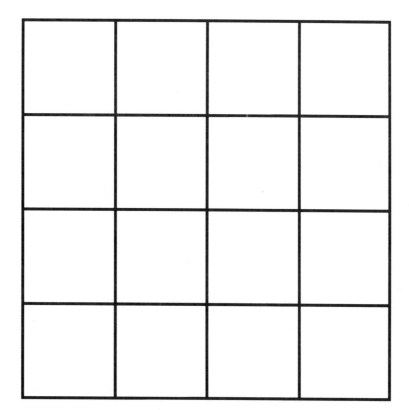

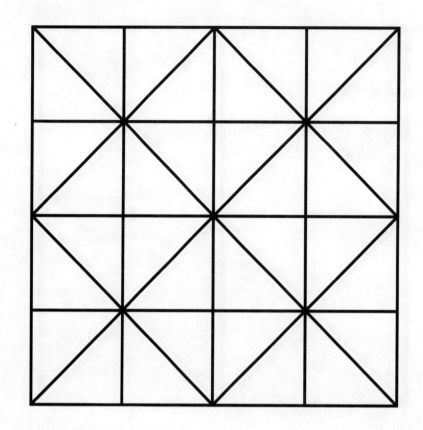

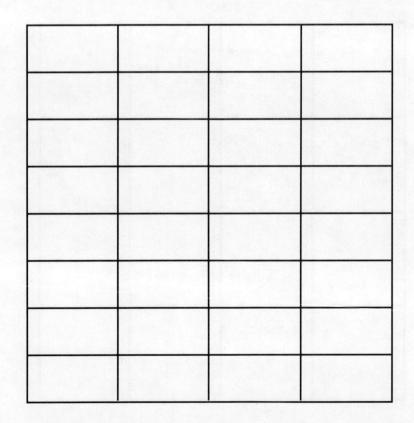

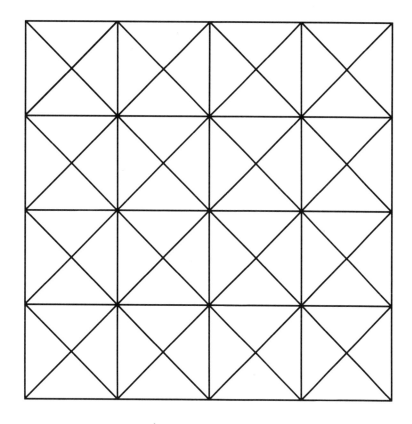

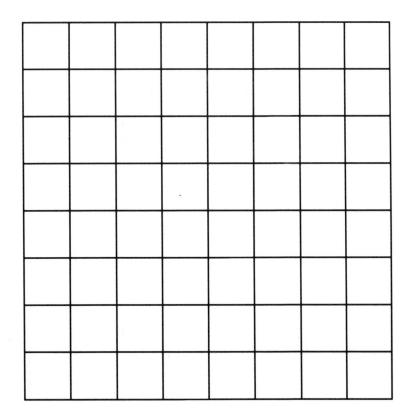

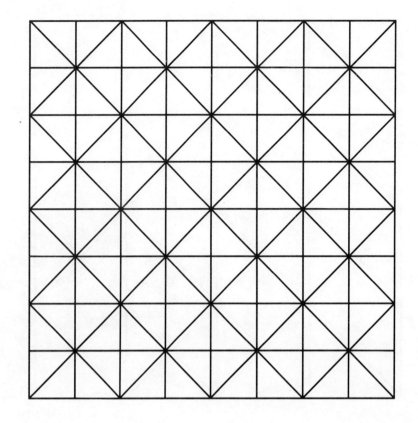

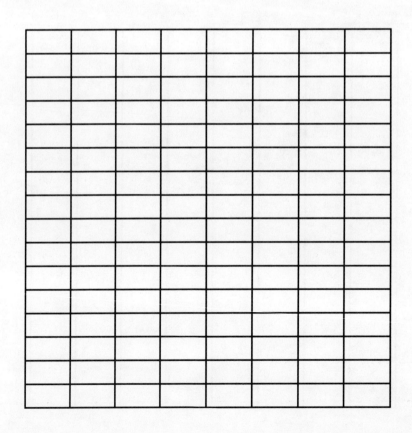

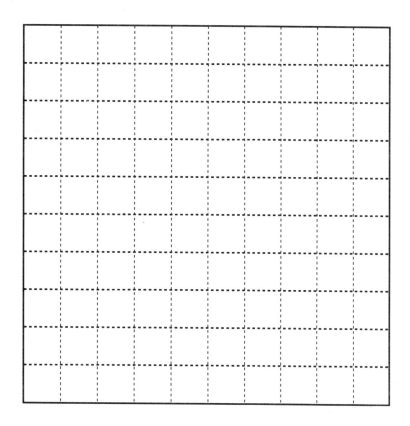

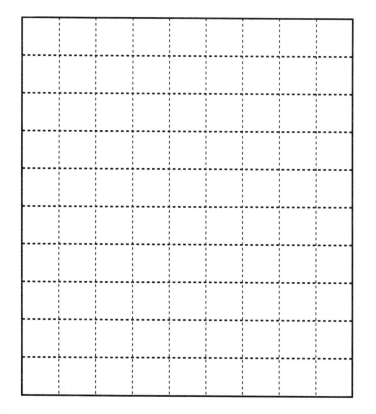

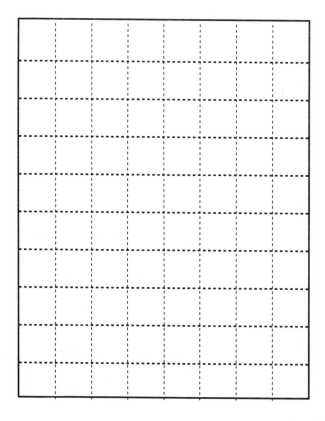

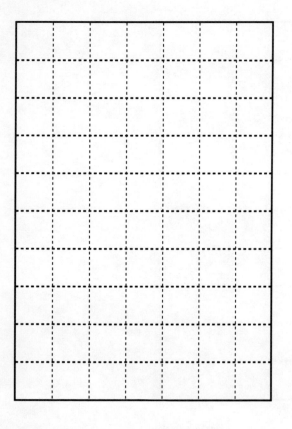
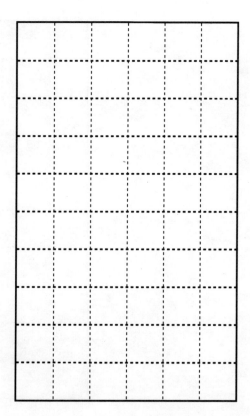
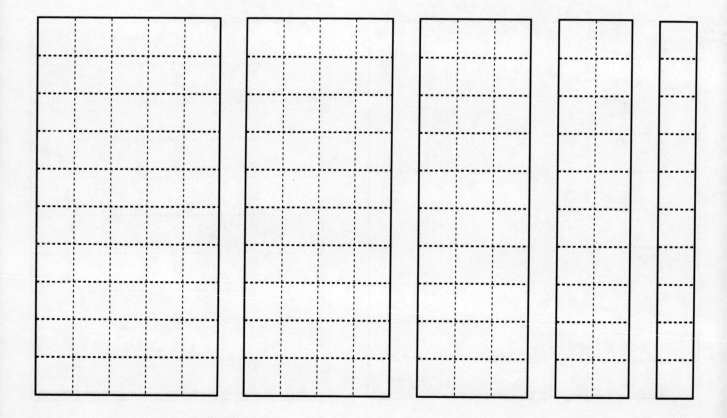

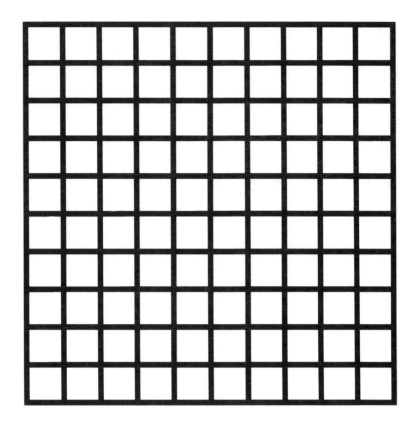

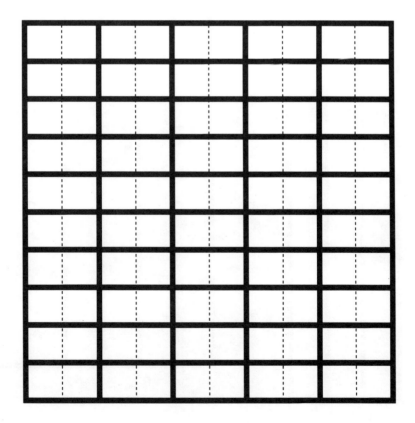

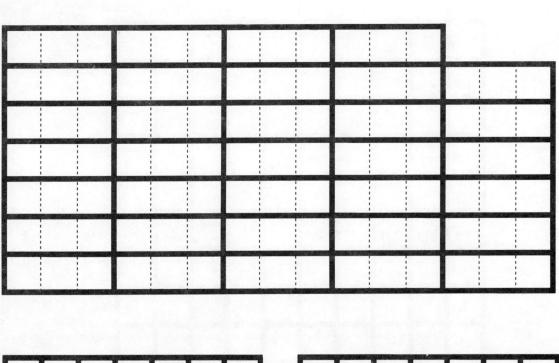

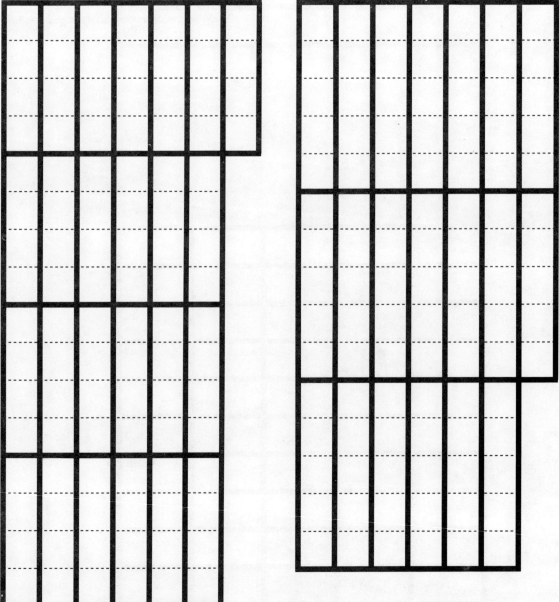

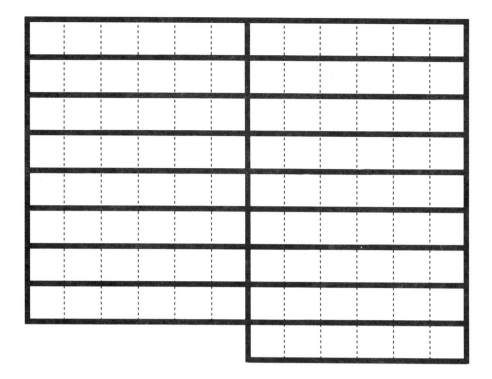

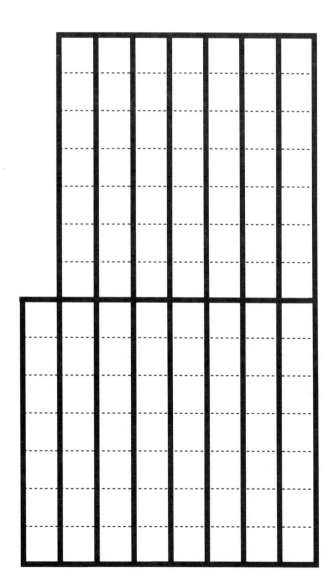

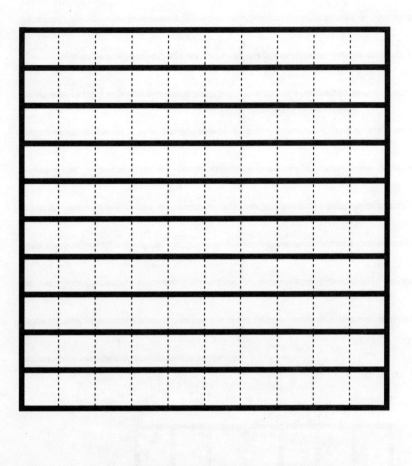

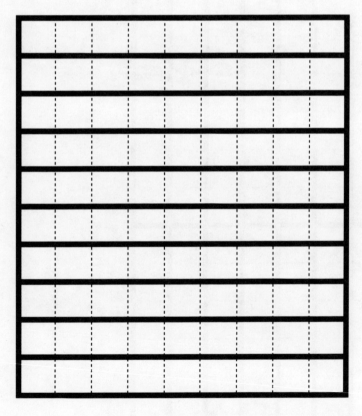

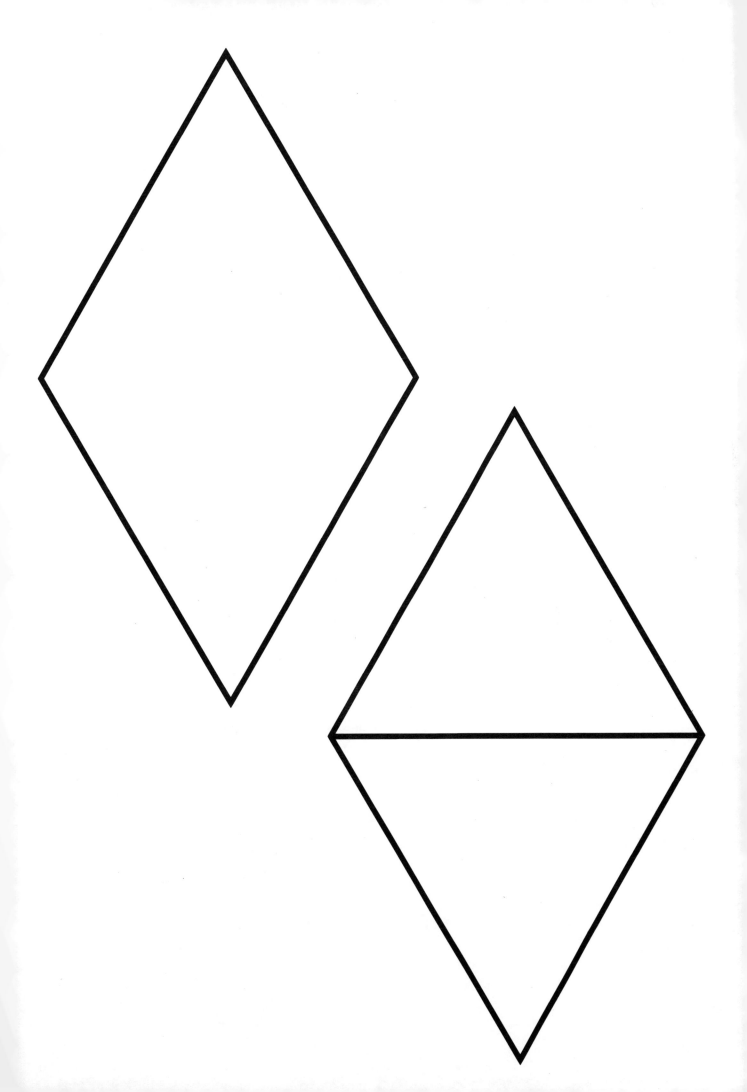

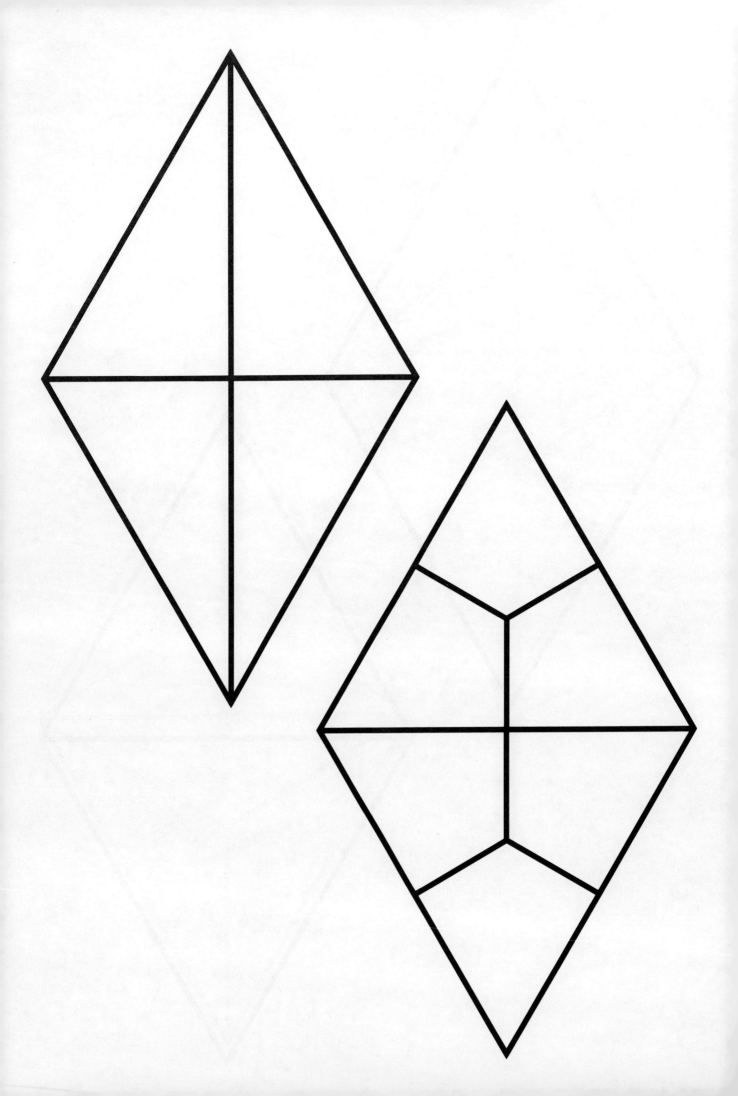

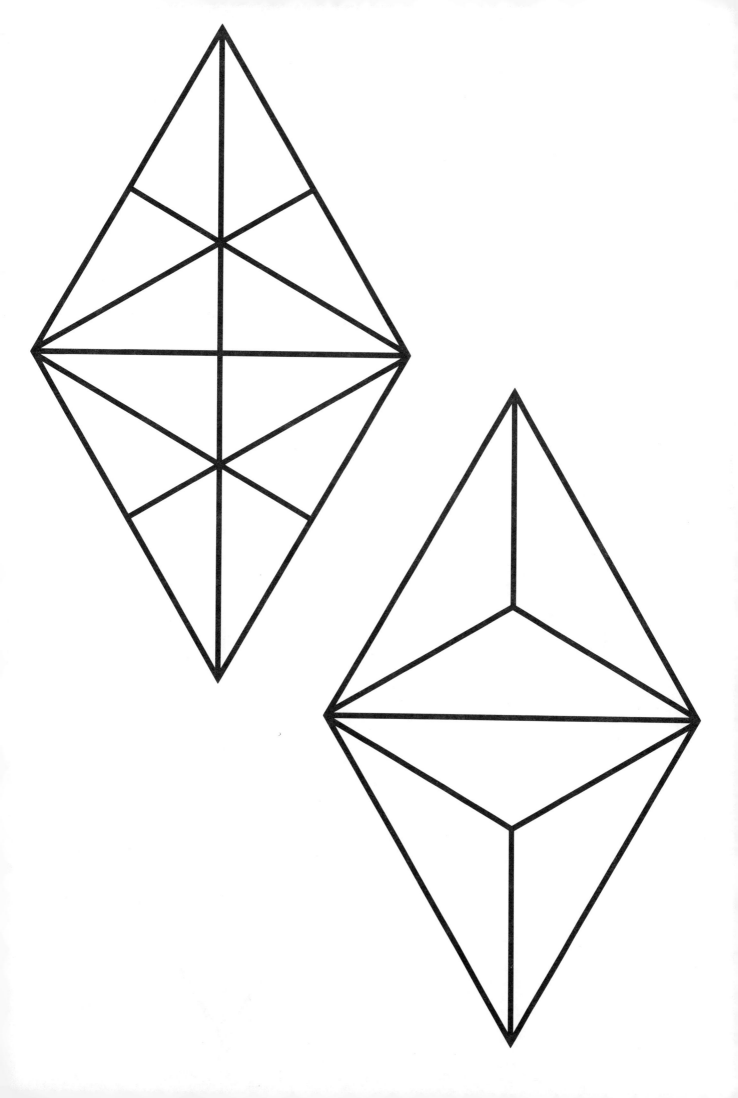

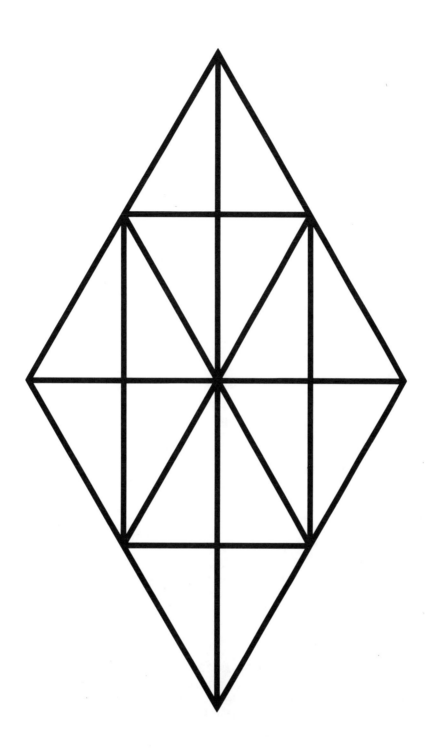

Books in this series

Rationale statement

The principles which govern this approach to mathematics teaching and learning are described in *Mapping mathematical meaning*. This theoretical statement provides the rationale for the way of teaching mathematics that is outlined in the other materials in this series.

Teaching and learning

Six topic books, *Base Ten*, *understanding the structure of the number system*; *Mathematics, a search for* **Patterns**; **Classification**, *a process for learning mathematics*; *Making sense of* **Fractions**; *The nature of* **Number**; and *Measuring Space*, give an account of these theories in action. These books are practical descriptions of activities and resources a teacher can use to establish a mathematical environment. They also discuss the types of response children make to such experiences, as well as map the development in children's mathematical thinking. Ongoing information about how to adapt and modify an activity to respond to children's developing thoughts provides the framework for continuity in learning. It also acts to challenge and support children's thinking beyond their existing parameters.

Managing the curriculum

A group of teachers implementing this approach have reflected on their classroom experiences. Their books provide practical information about how to manage aspects of the curriculum.

In these books, teachers share the structures and strategies they have developed to make the organisation and management of this approach to teaching effective and efficient.

Resourcing mathematics learning

In order to implement this way of teaching it is necessary to be well resourced. In particular, each child should have access to materials and activities which model the mathematics to be learnt. Many of these materials already exist in schools and are available from the various distributors of mathematics equipment. Sometimes teachers have needed to make their own resources to fit a specific task being set. To supplement the existing commercial supplies and, in the case of shape, to establish a more comprehensive set of examples, five books—*Triangles*; *Polygons*; *Fractions*; *Numbers and Numerals*; and *Dots and Grids*—provide pages which can be photocopied onto cardboard or paper, cut out and used to resource students' mathematics learning. They will save teachers the time and effort of making these resources for themselves.